BiG Thoughts for Little Thinkers

Heaven
By Joey Allen

New Leaf Press

First printing: June 2025

Copyright © 2025 by Joey Allen. All rights reserved. No part of this book may be reproduced, copied, broadcast, stored, or shared in any form whatsoever without written permission from the publisher, except in the case of brief quotations in articles and reviews. For information write:

New Leaf Press, P.O. Box 726, Green Forest, AR 72638

New Leaf Press is a division of the New Leaf Publishing Group, LLC.

ISBN: 978-0-89221-775-5

ISBN: 978-1-61458-933-4 (digital)

Library of Congress Control Number: 2025933625

Please consider requesting that a copy of this volume be purchased by your local library system.

Printed in China

Please visit our website for other great titles: www.newleafpress.com

For information regarding promotional opportunities, please contact the publicity department at pr@nlpg.com.

Illustrations and text by Joey Allen

For my son Joe IV

FOREWORD

Psalm 19 tells us the heavens declare God's glory and the skies proclaim what His hands have made. We just need to look up at night to behold God's creativity and majesty. As a child, night after night, even in the dead of winter, I'd look up through my telescope, into that magnificent sky. Sometimes on my back in my sleeping bag beside my Golden Retriever Champ, I'd count the meteors. Though I knew nothing of God, I sensed there must be something out there bigger than me.

Later, in my teens, I first heard the gospel. When I read about Jesus in a Bible someone gave me, I knew He was real. He became my Savior and Lord. I'd discovered that the "something bigger" was actually Some*one* bigger. Infinitely bigger.

When I was a child, I didn't have access to a beautiful, wonderful and biblically sound resource like Joey Allen's *Heaven*. But now you do. My hope is that this book will lead you and your children or grandchildren into the arms of our Savior.

May you and they and all of us together, look forward to the day when we—His people—along with His entire resurrected creation, will worship Him while talking and eating and playing and exploring and building with and for Him on the New Earth. I look forward to meeting you there!

Meanwhile, thank you, Joey, for this great book!

Randy Alcorn
Author of *Heaven* and *Happiness*

A WORD TO PARENTS AND TEACHERS

Jesus said, "Let the little children come to me, and do not hinder them, for the kingdom of heaven belongs to such as these" (Matthew 19:14; NIV). We have the opportunity to cultivate in children a joyful anticipation of Heaven. The Bible's teaching about Heaven can help children endure a world filled with difficulties and sorrow. As children grow up, they begin to wonder about death. What will happen when I die? What happened to Grandma or Grandpa? To these questions, the gospel provides a rich source of comfort and hope.

Many pious descriptions of Heaven are simply unappealing—sitting on clouds, strumming harps, endless Sunday school lessons. In contrast, the Bible's many descriptions of Heaven are exhilarating! The physical nature of Jesus' Resurrection means believers will enjoy immortality in an embodied existence in a real place, not a ghostly existence in an ephemeral nether sphere. The Bible describes the coming Kingdom of Heaven in concrete terms—but of course, the concrete in Heaven is gold!

Once, when my son was little, he made an inference in line with biblical teaching. He said, "In Heaven, sharks don't bite; they lick." His comment is consistent with Isaiah's prophecy, "The wolf and the lamb will graze together, and the lion will eat straw like the ox" (Isaiah 65:25; NASB). While scholars debate whether or not this prophecy refers to the Millennial Kingdom, we can be confident that such descriptions find perfect consummation in the eternal New Heavens and New Earth.

Let's encourage our children to look forward to the imminent return of the King of Heaven and to pray, "Come, Lord Jesus!" (Revelation 22:20).

Joey Allen
Chair of Missions and Evangelism, Midwestern Theological Seminary

Hi! My name is Celeste. I am so excited to tell you about an amazing place called "Heaven." God loves you and created you to spend forever with Him in Heaven.

John 3:16; 21:25; 1 John 4:10

In the beginning, God made the heavens and the earth. When God created the first humans, Adam and Eve, He put them in a beautiful place called "The Garden of Eden." Adam and Eve walked with God, loved each other, and peacefully lived with the animals. They cared for the garden and ruled over the world. Everything was very good.

Genesis 1-2

One day, Adam and Eve disobeyed God. They broke their perfect relationship with God, each other, and creation. That's when pain, sickness, and death entered the world, and Satan became the ruler of the world.

Genesis 3; John 12:31; 2 Corinthians 4:4; Ephesians 2:1-3; 6:12

Now, we are all sinners. We don't honor God the way we should. We are disobedient, selfish, and unloving. We sin with our words, thoughts, and actions. We deserve to be separated from God forever in a terrible place called "Hell."

Matthew 10:28; Romans 3:23;
2 Thessalonians 1:8-9; Revelation 21:8

God loved the world and promised to send a Savior. The Bible tells the true story of God's mission to crush Satan and get rid of sin and death. God plans to make the world even better than it began.

Genesis 3:15; John 3:16; Romans 16:20; Revelation 21:5

At just the right time, God the Father sent His Son Jesus to be the Savior. Jesus left Heaven and came down to Earth. Jesus taught His followers about the Kingdom of Heaven and how to live as citizens of Heaven.

Matthew 5–7; 2 Corinthians 8:9; Galatians 4:4; Philippians 3:20; 1 John 4:14

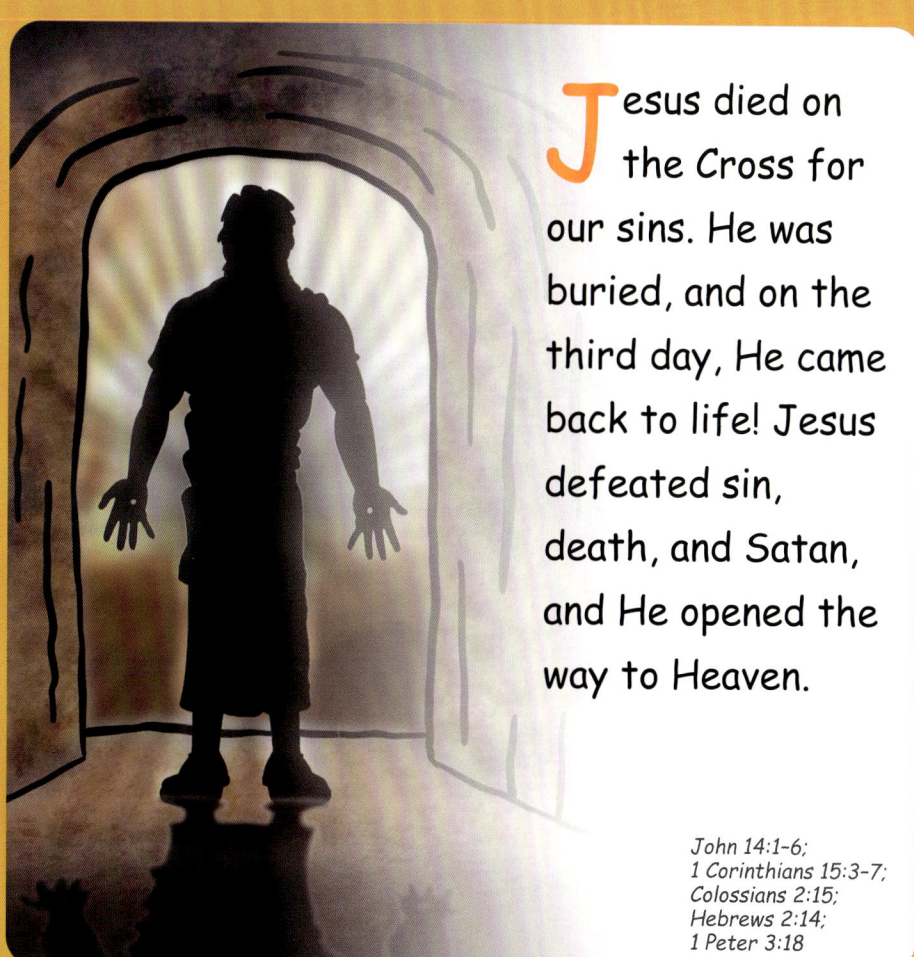

Jesus died on the Cross for our sins. He was buried, and on the third day, He came back to life! Jesus defeated sin, death, and Satan, and He opened the way to Heaven.

*John 14:1-6;
1 Corinthians 15:3-7;
Colossians 2:15;
Hebrews 2:14;
1 Peter 3:18*

After Jesus came back to life, He had a new, glorified, perfect, and healthy body, but His friends could still recognize Him and touch Him. Jesus talked with them, and they ate food together. Then Jesus went back to Heaven.

Luke 24:37-43; John 20:18-20; 26-29; Acts 1:9

Right now, Jesus is in Heaven. He is preparing our forever home. One day, He will come back and bring Heaven to Earth. He will make all things new, and believers will live with Him in the New Heaven and New Earth.

Isaiah 65:17;
John 14:1-4; 16:22; 18:36;
Hebrews 11:10;
2 Peter 3:11-13;
Revelation 21:5

Many people think good people go to Heaven and bad people go to Hell, but no one is good enough to go to Heaven. Sin makes your heart dirty, and you can't clean yourself. Only Jesus can make you clean.

Psalm 14:1-3; Isaiah 64:6; Jeremiah 17:9; Romans 6:23; Ephesians 2:8-9; Titus 3:5

Jesus forgives everyone who trusts in Him alone. When you trust in Him, He gives you the Holy Spirit and makes you a child of God. If you are connected to Jesus, you can go where He is—Heaven!

John 1:12; 14:3; 2 Corinthians 5:8; Ephesians 1:3-14

Have you ever wondered what Heaven will be like? Think of the best place you can possibly imagine. Now, think: Heaven will be even better.

Ephesians 3:20–21

The Bible tells us many things about Heaven, but it doesn't tell us everything we'd like to know. It is OK to imagine Heaven but remember: It will be *better* than your best dreams.

Hebrews 11:14–16

When we think about what life will be like in Heaven, we are like caterpillars trying to imagine life as a butterfly. For those who trust in Jesus, the future will be amazing!

1 Corinthians 15:35-54

This world is a shadow of the world to come. The New Heaven and New Earth are more real than this world because they will last forever.

2 Corinthians 4:18; Colossians 2:17; Hebrews 8:5; 1 John 2:17

The New Heaven and New Earth will have everything you love about Earth without anything bad. It will be so much better because there will be no sin, sickness, selfishness, or sadness.

Revelation 7:16–17; 21:4

Learning about the Garden of Eden gives us a picture of what the New Heaven and New Earth will be like. Not only will there be a beautiful garden, but there will also be a city called New Jerusalem. The city walls are made of jewels, the streets are gold, and a beautiful river runs through it. A fruit tree grows on both sides of the river.

Isaiah 65:18-19; Revelation 21:2; 15-21; 22:1-2

If you are God's child, you do not have to fear death because He will bring you back to life. He will give you a real, glorified body like the body Jesus has. You will not be an angel or a ghost. You will be more *you* than you've ever been. You will be the person God created you to be—perfect, healthy, beautiful, and loving.

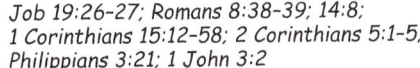

Job 19:26-27; Romans 8:38-39; 14:8;
1 Corinthians 15:12-58; 2 Corinthians 5:1-5;
Philippians 3:21; 1 John 3:2

In Heaven, there is no more darkness, crying, or pain. You will be free from sin and temptation. God will rescue you from every selfish desire and make everything right. You will perfectly love and serve God and other people.

Revelation 7:15; 21:4, 23-27; 22:3-5

When you get to Heaven, you will meet Jesus in person. You will also meet all of the believers who came before you—people like Abraham and Sarah, Moses, Rahab, David, Daniel, and Esther. In Heaven, you will meet many people from all over the world.

Hebrews 11;
Revelation 7:9; 22:4

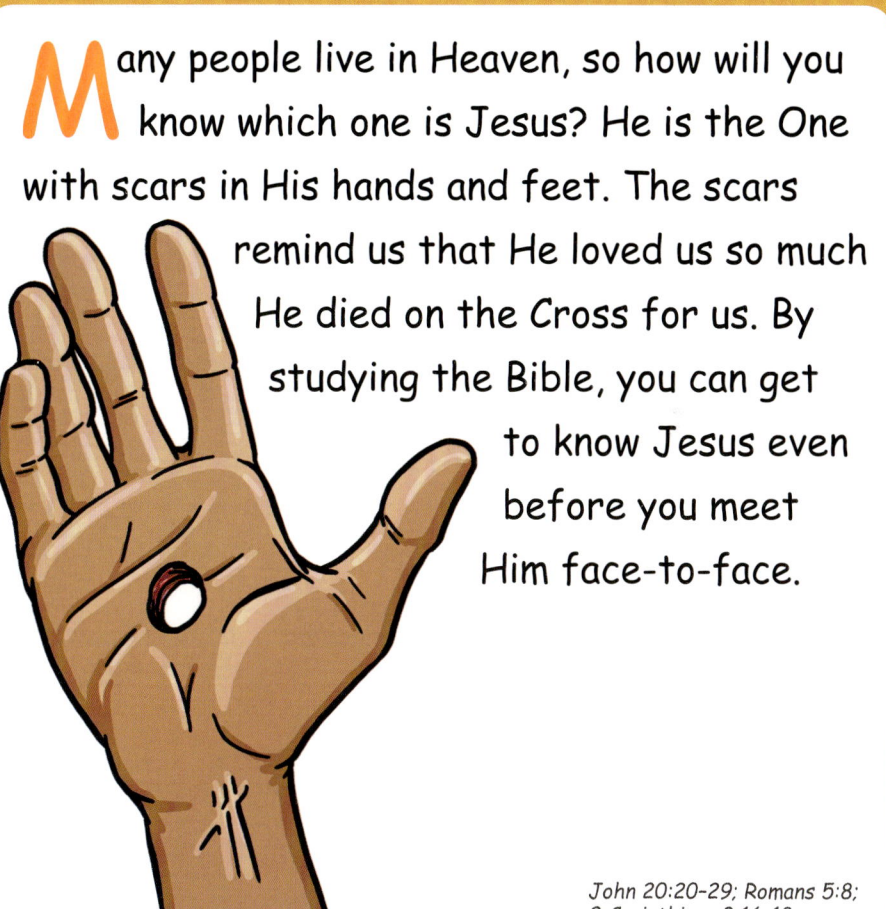

Many people live in Heaven, so how will you know which one is Jesus? He is the One with scars in His hands and feet. The scars remind us that He loved us so much He died on the Cross for us. By studying the Bible, you can get to know Jesus even before you meet Him face-to-face.

*John 20:20-29; Romans 5:8;
2 Corinthians 3:16-18*

How you live on Earth matters forever. The happiest people in Heaven are those who trust and obey God on Earth and invite others to join them in Heaven.

John 14:21
1 Corinthians 3:11-15;
2 Corinthians 5:9-11;
Galatians 6:7-9;
Colossians 3:23-24

God promises to reward His children who love and serve Him. God gives different kinds of rewards. He gives joy, crowns, and the chance to rule with Him over His Kingdom. Wouldn't you like to hear Him say to you, "Well done, my good and faithful servant"?

Matthew 6:19-20; 10:42; 25:23; Luke 14:14; 1 Corinthians 3:8; 2 Corinthians 5:10; Ephesians 6:7-8; Colossians 3:23-24; 2 Timothy 4:8; Revelation 3:21; 20:6; 22:12

You will never be bored in Heaven. God is infinite, so there will always be more to discover about Him. The more you know God, the more you will love and worship Him. Heaven will always keep getting better and better and better.

2 Corinthians 3:18; Ephesians 2:6-7; 2 Peter 3:18; Revelation 21:5

In Heaven, we will worship God in many different ways. We will sing songs, dance, and make music. We will spend time with loved ones, make new friends, laugh, play, and tell stories. We will eat delicious food, learn cool things, explore the New Heaven and New Earth, rest, and build amazing stuff. We will have so much fun!

Psalm 104:33; Isaiah 65:21; Matthew 8:11; Luke 22:30; Hebrews 4:1-13; Revelation 2:7; 5:9-10; 14:3; 19:9; 22:3-5

The Bible says that one day, every bird, land animal, and sea creature will praise God. The Bible mentions different kinds of animals that will be in the New Heaven and New Earth, such as horses, bears, lions, lambs, and leopards. Dinosaurs will probably be there, too!

Romans 8:19–22; Isaiah 11:6–9; Revelation 5:13; 19:14

If you know that Heaven is your forever home, you can live generously and without fear during your short time on Earth. While we wait for Jesus to return, we should introduce other people to Him so they can worship Jesus with us in Heaven.

Matthew 28:18-20
2 Timothy 4:18; Titus 2:11-14

In Heaven, you'll be with your forever family in your forever home, but the best part will be praising God the Father, rejoicing in the Holy Spirit, and enjoying the Lord Jesus forever! I can hardly wait!

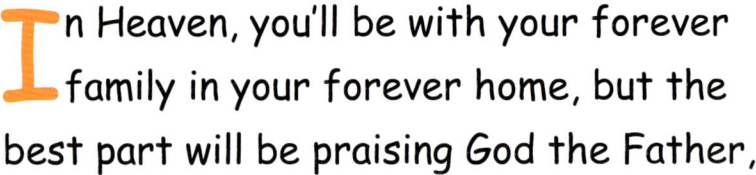

*Psalm 16:11; John 17:3;
2 Corinthians 13:14;
1 Thessalonians 4:13-18;
Revelation 22:3-4, 17, 20*